INSPIRE

HALLE BAILEY

BY MARY BLECKWEHL

AMICUS LEARNING

Inspire is published by
Amicus Learning, an imprint of Amicus
P.O. Box 227
Mankato, MN 56002
www.amicuspublishing.us

Editor: Ana Brauer
Series Designer: Kathleen Petelinsek
Book Designer and Photo Researcher: Emily Dietz

Library of Congress Cataloging-in-Publication Data
Names: Bleckwehl, Mary E., author.
Title: Halle Bailey / by Mary Bleckwehl.
Description: Mankato, MN : Amicus Learning, 2025. | Series: Inspire | Includes bibliographical references and index. | Audience: Ages 5–9 | Audience: Grades 2–3 | Summary: "Learn about singer and actress Halle Bailey and her journey to Hollywood in this biography packed with photos and fun facts suitable for young readers. Includes a table of contents, glossary, further resources, and index" —Provided by publisher.
Identifiers: LCCN 2024012079 (print) | LCCN 2024012080 (ebook) | ISBN 9798892001021 (library binding) | ISBN 9798892001601 (paperback) | ISBN 9798892002189 (ebook)
Subjects: LCSH: Bailey, Halle, 2000—Juvenile literature. | Singers—United States—Biography—Juvenile literature. | Actors—United States—Biography—Juvenile literature.
Classification: LCC ML3930.B206 B54 2025 (print) | LCC ML3930.B206 (ebook) | DDC 782.42164092 [B]—dc23/eng/20240315
LC record available at https://lccn.loc.gov/2024012079
LC ebook record available at https://lccn.loc.gov/2024012080

Photo Credits: Alamy Stock Photo/Album, 17, Collection Christophel, 5; Associated Press/Jordan Strauss, cover; Getty Images/Alberto E. Rodriguez, 12, Jesse Grant, 16, Jerod Harris, 19, Kate Green, 20, Larry Busacca/PW18, 15, Lester Cohen, 6, Michael S. Schwartz, 10–11, William Gottlieb, 9; Shutterstock/Luca Perra, 14, M.E. Mulder, 8, New Africa, 13, Ruslan Ivantsov, 13

Printed in China

Table of Contents

A Part of Her World

Actress Halle Bailey dives into the water. She twirls. She glides. Her mermaid outfit shimmers. Spotlights make the movie set look magical. But it is Bailey's singing that steals the show. Bailey is a singer and actress.

Halle Bailey plays Ariel in Disney's *The Little Mermaid* (2023).

Halle Bailey (right) is two years younger than her sister, Chloe Bailey.

Do-It-Yourself Kid

Bailey loves music. As a kid, she wrote songs with her older sister, Chloe. The first songs they wrote were horrible. But they got better. She and Chloe liked learning on their own. They learned to play guitar and piano from YouTube videos.

Inspiration

When Bailey was five, she listened to a pink CD. It was by jazz singer Billie Holiday. Holiday's music style **inspired** her to try new ideas. She is one of Bailey's biggest music influences.

GUITAR HEROES

Bailey enjoys playing the guitar. She is a fan of guitarists Jimi Hendrix and Lenny Kravitz.

Billie Holiday is one of the most famous female jazz singers of all time.

Bailey (left) sings with Chloe at an event for Radio Disney in 2012.

Sisterhood

At age 11, Bailey and her sister had a plan. They sang and recorded famous songs. They posted **song covers** to YouTube. This was the start of the Chloe x Halle **duo**. Soon, they were a hit!

Chloe X Halle won the fifth season of *Radio Disney's Next Big Thing* in 2012.

Family Matters

Bailey's parents knew she had talent. Her father became her manager. When she was 12, her family moved from Georgia to Los Angeles, California. This put Bailey in the heart of the music scene.

SONGWRITING DAD

Bailey's father helped teach her how to write songs when she was eight.

A Huge Break

In 2013, the girls posted a Beyoncé song. The video went **viral**. Beyoncé heard it and loved their singing. She offered them a recording contract in 2015. In 2018, the sisters were the opening act for Beyoncé's tour: *On the Run II*.

FAMOUS FAN
In 2016, First Lady Michelle Obama invited the Bailey sisters to perform at the White House.

Bailey (right) and her sister became popular when they sang the Beyoncé song "Pretty Hurts."

In 2023, Bailey attended the world premiere of *The Little Mermaid*.

Making a Splash

Bailey played Ariel in the 2023 movie, *The Little Mermaid.* She worked hard to get in shape for the part. Every muscle needed to be strong. It took months of training. The role made Bailey a Disney princess!

MOVIE STAR
Bailey appeared in the movie musical *The Color Purple* later in 2023.

Going Solo

Bailey spent years singing with her sister. They acted together, too. They played twins on the show *Grown-ish*. Now, they both have solo careers.

Bailey's **debut** song, *Angel*, came out in 2023. The song was nominated for a Grammy!

As of 2024, Bailey has been nominated for six Grammy Awards.

Bailey has become an inspiration to young girls all over the world.

The Future

In 2024, Bailey said she plans to make new music with her sister. Bailey loves to try new things. She has just begun as a solo artist. Her career continues to grow. Her family cheers her on. She hopes to do the same for others.

SUPER STATS

HALLE BAILEY

Birthday: March 27, 2000

Hometowns: Mableton, GA and Los Angeles, CA

Birthplace: Atlanta, GA

Children: 1

Acting Roles: *The Little Mermaid* (2023), *The Color Purple* (2023), *Grown-ish* (2018–2022)

AWARDS

Best Actress in a Motion Picture from Bulletin Awards: 2023

Gamechanger of the Year from Glamour Awards: 2023

Ensemble Award-Film from Celebration of Cinema and Television: 2023

GLOSSARY

debut A person's first performance on stage or on film.

duo A pair; two people.

inspire To motivate a person to want to do something.

song cover A new recording of a song by someone other than the original performer.

viral Quickly and widely spread or made popular by people sharing on the internet.

READ MORE

Poux, Jennifer. **Chloe X Halle.** Grosset & Dunlap, 2020.

Stevenson, Robin. **Kid Musicians: True Tales of Childhood from Entertainers, Songwriters, and Stars.** Quirk Books, 2024.

ON THE WEB

Chloe x Halle YouTube
https://www.youtube.com/channel/UCKvu7JgqK7-ZKUKHC33meEw

Halle Bailey
https://www.britannica.com/biography/Halle-Bailey

Introducing Halle Bailey
https://halle-bailey.com/

INDEX

About the Author

Mary Bleckwehl is a children's author who loves cookie dough and talking to kids. She is happiest when she is biking and exploring new places. Mary lives in Minnesota with her husband and monster dog. Check out her books at marybleckwehl.com.